AR Quiz # 119318
Level 2.0 LG
Points 0.5   410L

Pebble®

Persian Cats

by **Wendy Perkins**

Consulting Editor: Gail Saunders-Smith, PhD

Consultant: Jennifer Zablotny, DVM
Member, American Veterinary Medical Association

Capstone
press®
Mankato, Minnesota

Pebble Books are published by Capstone Press,
151 Good Counsel Drive, P.O. Box 669, Mankato, Minnesota 56002.
www.capstonepress.com

1 2 3 4 5 6 13 12 11 10 09 08

Library of Congress Cataloging-in-Publication Data
Perkins, Wendy, 1957–
 Persian cats / by Wendy Perkins.
 p. cm. — (Pebble Books. Cats)
 Includes bibliographical references and index.
 ISBN-13: 978-1-4296-1218-0 (hardcover)
 ISBN-10: 1-4296-1218-5 (hardcover)
 1. Persian cat — Juvenile literature. I. Title. II. Series.
SF449.P4P47 2008
636.8'3 — dc22   2007017795

Summary: Simple text and photographs present an introduction to the Persian breed,
its growth from kitten to adult, and pet care information.

Note to Parents and Teachers

The Cats set supports national science standards related to life
science. This book describes and illustrates Persian cats. The images
support early readers in understanding the text. The repetition of
words and phrases helps early readers learn new words. This book
also introduces early readers to subject-specific vocabulary words,
which are defined in the Glossary section. Early readers may need
assistance to read some words and to use the Table of Contents,
Glossary, Read More, Internet Sites, and Index sections of the book.

Table of Contents

Quiet Cats

Persians are the most popular cat breed. Many people own these quiet, gentle cats.

Say it like this:
Persian
(PUR-zhuhn)

Persian cats have
small, flat noses.

Persians are fluffy.
Light, silky fur covers
a short undercoat.

From Kitten to Adult

Newborn Persians
have very short fur.
They stay close to their
mothers to keep warm.

At six weeks, kittens
are fluffy and playful.
They learn to lick
their fur to keep it clean.

14

Kittens grow quickly.
Adult Persians can weigh
as much as 15 pounds
(7 kilograms).

Caring for Persians

Persians need to stay inside. Their fine fur doesn't keep them warm in cold weather.

A Persian's fur can clump together and become matted. Persians need to be combed every day.

Persians like attention from their owners. They love sitting on laps and being petted.

Glossary

attention — playing, talking, and spending time with a person or animal

breed — a certain kind of animal within an animal group

fine — thin

gentle — kind and calm

mat — a thick, tangled bunch of hair

popular — liked or enjoyed by many people

silky — smooth and soft

undercoat — the short fur underneath a Persian's long, fine fur

Read More

Barnes, Julia. *Pet Cats.* Pet Pals. Milwaukee: Gareth Stevens, 2007.

Murray, Julie. *Persian Cats.* A Buddy Book. Animal Kingdom. Edina, Minn.: Abdo, 2005.

Shores, Erika L. *Caring for Your Cat.* First Facts. Postively Pets. Mankato, Minn.: Capstone Press, 2007.

Internet Sites

FactHound offers a safe, fun way to find Internet sites related to this book. All of the sites on FactHound have been researched by our staff.

Here's how:

1. Visit *www.facthound.com*

2. Choose your grade level.

3. Type in this book **ID 1429612185** for age-appropriate sites. You may also browse subjects by clicking on letters, or by clicking on pictures and words.

4. Click on the **Fetch It** button.

FactHound will fetch the best sites for you!

Index

Word Count: 122
Grade: 1
Early-Intervention Level: 16

Editorial Credits
Erika L. Shores, editor; Renée T. Doyle, set designer; Veronica Bianchini and Ted Williams, contributing designers; Linda Clavel, photo researcher

Photo Credits
Fiona Green, 6, 16, 20
iStockphoto/David Kelly, cover, 1, 22
Norvia Behling, 10, 12, 18
Peter Arnold/Schulte, M., 8
Shutterstock/Suzanne Tucker, 4, 14